CW01084628

Original title:
Dreams on the Wind

Author: Derek Caldwell
ISBN HARDBACK: 978-9916-90-612-5
ISBN PAPERBACK: 978-9916-90-613-2

# Melodies Caressed by the Sky

Whispers of clouds drift soft and low,
Their gentle tune, a sweetened flow.
Breezes carry tales in flight,
Dreams unfold in morning light.

Colors dance on wings of grace,
Nature's voice, a warm embrace.
Every note, a tender sigh,
Melodies caressed by the sky.

Stars will blink with secret glee,
As night falls, a symphony.
Strings of silver, dreams awake,
Echoes soft, for joy's sweet sake.

In twilight's glow, the world does sway,
Harmonies at close of day.
With every heartbeat, we belong,
To this timeless, endless song.

## The Flight of Unnamed Wishes

Upon the wind, they drift away,
Silent hopes in soft ballet.
Carried high on feathered dreams,
Like whispers caught in moonlit beams.

In twilight's hush, they seek the stars,
Soaring high past earthly bars.
Courage born of fragile light,
The flight of unnamed wishes bright.

Time can weave its gentle thread,
Binding tales of words unsaid.
In each embrace, a wish fulfilled,
Hearts take wing, unbound, unstilled.

As dawn's blush paints skies anew,
Fragments dance on morning dew.
With every dawn, new dreams arise,
The flight of wishes in the skies.

## Breezes that Unravel Time

Whispers dance on gentle air,
Carrying tales of ages past.
Moments drift, both light and rare,
In breezes soft, our dreams are cast.

Fleeting thoughts on currents glide,
Echoes of a life well-spent.
In twilight's glow, we take our ride,
To realms where time and space relent.

## Canvas of the Celestial

Stars brush strokes on velvet night,
Painting worlds with silver sheen.
Galaxies swirl in cosmic flight,
Whispers of what might have been.

Planets spin in graceful dance,
Each a tale of heat and cold.
In silence, we take our chance,
To dream of stories yet untold.

## Kites Made of Wishes

Up they soar on strings of hope,
Carried high by winds of fate.
Colorful dreams on the slope,
Each a symbol, never late.

With every tug, the sky replies,
Gifting flight to hearts that dare.
Beneath the endless, sprawling skies,
In the azure, wishes flare.

## The Airy Realm of Reverie

In soft clouds, our thoughts ignite,
Floating high, they twist and twirl.
In daydreams bright, we find delight,
In visions spun, our spirits whirl.

Drifting far from earthly cares,
With every breath, the magic blooms.
Through light and laughter, life declares,
In reverie, our heart resumes.

## Infinite Musings Above

Beneath the vast and endless sky,
Thoughts drift like clouds that wander by.
Whispers of dreams in currents soar,
Each moment crafted, forevermore.

Past the horizon where secrets dwell,
A place where stories weave and swell.
Time drifts softly like a feather,
In the embrace of the endless tether.

## Reverberations in the Calm Air

The stillness sings in gentle tones,
Echoes of life in soft vibrations moans.
A tranquil breeze weaves through the trees,
Carrying whispers with elegant ease.

In the hush, the world holds its breath,
Moments linger, flaring with depth.
The dance of silence, pure and sublime,
Paints the essence of fragile time.

## Horizon Chasers and Skyward Seekers

Eager hearts leap toward the unknown,
Footsteps echo on paths unshown.
With eyes like fire, they seek the light,
Chasing shadows that blend with night.

Beyond each rise, a promise awaits,
Adventures unfold as courage dictates.
Boundless journeys, wild and free,
Unlocking the chains of destiny.

### The Kaleidoscope of Airborne Whims

Colors swirl in a playful dance,
Dreams take flight, given a chance.
With laughter carried on the breeze,
Imagination blooms like vibrant trees.

Each turn reveals a brand new view,
Resplendent tapestries of every hue.
In the sky's embrace, freedom sings,
A symphony born of whimsical things.

# A Canvas of Fleeing Fantasies

Whispers dance on the breeze,
Dreams painted with soft hues.
A canvas stretched wide and free,
Fading fast, as night sneaks through.

Tomorrow holds a brighter shade,
Yet shadows linger, dark and deep.
In the twilight, memories fade,
While stars above quietly weep.

## Horizons of Hope and Light

Beneath the dawn's first gentle ray,
Hope awakens, warm and bright.
A promise made with each new day,
In the glow of morning's light.

Clouds may gather, storms may rise,
Yet love remains, a guiding star.
With every dream, we touch the skies,
Our spirits soaring, near and far.

## Restless Spirits in Flight

Wings unfurl on winds of change,
Restless hearts seek paths unknown.
In the night, the wild call strange,
To wander, drift, no longer alone.

Each heartbeat drums a whispered song,
Echoes calling from afar.
With every step, we find where we belong,
Chasing shadows, seeking the stars.

## The Breath of the Universe

In every heart, a heartbeat flows,
The universe breathes in and out.
With every pulse, the cosmos glows,
A sacred dance, a timeless route.

Stars align in velvet skies,
Whispers carried on the night.
In silence, unspoken ties,
We find our place, we find our light.

## Shadows of Infinity

In twilight's grasp, the shadows creep,
They weave a tale, both dark and deep.
In whispered winds, the secrets flow,
Embracing dreams that ebb and glow.

Through endless night, the silence sings,
Of ancient paths and mystic rings.
A dance of stars in velvet skies,
Where time, it bends, and never dies.

## Vagabond Thoughts under Moonlight

Beneath the moon, my heart takes flight,
Wandering through the veil of night.
Each thought a star, a fleeting spark,
Guiding me through the endless dark.

Footsteps echo on silent trails,
Whispers of love in the night winds' sails.
I chase the dreams of far-off lands,
With every breath, the world expands.

## The Breath of Forgotten Journeys

In echoes of time, past trips still call,
Whispers of laughter, a lovely thrall.
The scent of earth, the touch of sky,
Each heartbeat sings of days gone by.

Memories dance in the fading light,
Carried on winds that once felt right.
Longing for roads that stretched so far,
Guided by hope, like a wandering star.

## Starlit Aspirations

Under the vastness, dreams ignite,
Each twinkling star, a wish in flight.
Hope paints the canvas of the night,
Guiding hearts towards the light.

With every breath, ambitions rise,
Chasing the glow of distant skies.
We weave our fates, we write our songs,
In starlit realms, where each belongs.

# Paths Woven with Invisible Air

Gentle whispers guide the way,
Through the leaves where children play.
Sunlight dances on the ground,
In the silence, dreams are found.

Footsteps echo in the mist,
Each adventure, none dismissed.
With every turn, new worlds awake,
In the fabric that we make.

Voices blending with the breeze,
Carving pathways through the trees.
Starlit nights and golden dawns,
Paths unfold like hidden fawns.

We journey on, forever bright,
Woven paths of purest light.
With invisible threads we roam,
In the air, we find our home.

## Shadows Gliding Past Reality

Beneath the glow of twilight's veil,
Shadows dance, their whispers pale.
Formless figures glide and sway,
Woven stories to convey.

Fleeting echoes drift in time,
Secrets held in every rhyme.
Through the darkness, light shall gleam,
Awakening a shared dream.

Footsteps linger, softly traced,
Moments shared, yet unchased.
In the twilight's gentle art,
Shadows play a vital part.

Reality and dreams collide,
In the spaces where we hide.
Catching glimpses, truths unspun,
As shadows claim the setting sun.

## A Reverberation of Tomorrow

In the pulse of dawn's embrace,
Hope emerges, a gentle grace.
Each heartbeat whispers what will come,
In the silence, life's hum.

Golden rays break through the night,
Promises wrapped in purest light.
Echoes of dreams, alive and free,
Tomorrow's song calls to me.

Winds of change caress the soul,
Guiding paths to a greater goal.
With every second, futures grow,
In the dance of ebb and flow.

A reverberation deep and clear,
Tomorrow's hope, forever near.
In the tapestry of time,
We weave our dreams in every rhyme.

# Supernova of the Heart

In the depths where passions burn,
A supernova waits its turn.
Exploding colors, fierce and bright,
Igniting worlds with pure delight.

Feel the heat of love's embrace,
A cosmic dance, a timeless grace.
Every heartbeat, a star's ignite,
Stealing shadows, embracing light.

In the void where silence reigns,
Hope's radiance breaks all chains.
A universe within us stirs,
As love defies the dark detours.

From this heart, the cosmos streams,
Supernova of our dreams.
Together we burn, one heart, one flame,
In this vast expanse, forever the same.

## The Gift of Airborne Aspirations

In the sky, dreams take flight,
Whispers of hope in the night.
Each breeze carries a soft tale,
Of lives set free, they shall not fail.

Clouds unfold their gentle grace,
Guided by an unseen trace.
Hearts ascend with every breath,
Embracing life, defying death.

Listen close to winds that sigh,
Promises held in the vast sky.
With each leap, we claim our share,
The world is ours, beyond compare.

Free our souls, let courage soar,
With every heartbeat, we explore.
The gift of air, bright and rare,
Awakens dreams beyond despair.

## Airborne Visions of Tomorrow

In the morn, horizons gleam,
Visions dance in whispered dream.
Up we go, no chains to bind,
In the breeze, new paths we find.

Colors blend in sunlight's grace,
Chasing shadows, we embrace.
Futures drawn in skies above,
Lift our hearts on wings of love.

A canvas wide, we paint our fate,
Every heartbeat, we create.
With open minds, we chase the light,
Airborne visions set us right.

Fear dissolves like clouds of gray,
In the dawn, we find our way.
Each hopeful heart, a soaring kite,
Together, we'll ascend the height.

# Glimmers of a Sweet Escape

Stars ignite the velvet night,
Glimmers shine, a pure delight.
Fragrant dreams on zephyrs ride,
In this moment, hope won't hide.

From the ground, we long to break,
Find our peace, the road we take.
Softly now, the shadows creep,
In the silence, secrets keep.

Waves of laughter fill the air,
Memories, bright and rare.
Through the night, we'll find our grace,
A sweet escape, a warm embrace.

In the stillness, hearts collide,
With each breath, we turn the tide.
Trust the winds to lead the way,
To tomorrow's bright and golden day.

## The Tides of Wandering Hopes

Waves of change roll on the shore,
Each retreat opens a door.
Hopes like feathers drift and glide,
On the ocean, dreams abide.

Salt and wind, a timeless song,
In their rhythm, we belong.
Sands of time shift far and wide,
With every tide, our souls will ride.

Journey forth with spirits free,
Let the currents guide your plea.
In the depths, find treasures rare,
In the tide, our hearts laid bare.

With each swell, we rise and fall,
Wandering hopes, we hear their call.
Embrace the waves, let them sway,
In the dance, we find our way.

## Serenity in Flight

In the hush of dawn's embrace,
Wings spread wide, a gentle grace.
Above the world, I find my way,
In the arms of sky, I drift and play.

Clouds whisper secrets soft and light,
A dance of dreams in tranquil flight.
I leave the weight of earth behind,
In solace found, my heart unwinds.

Through azure seas and golden hue,
The winds of change bring visions new.
Each breath a gift, a fleeting chance,
In every rise, I hear love's dance.

As stars begin to wink and shine,
I soar through realms where spirits climb.
With every glide, my soul takes wing,
Embraced by peace, my heart can sing.

## Tales Carried by the Gales

Stories woven in the breeze,
Carried far with perfect ease.
Whispers echo, tales unfold,
Of heroes brave and journeys bold.

From mountain high to ocean wide,
The gales bear witness, none can hide.
Each breath a tale from times gone by,
In twilight's glow, the shadows fly.

Rustling leaves in the evening glow,
Share secrets only nature knows.
With every gust, a heart-shaped lore,
Of love and loss, forevermore.

Across the fields, through ancient stone,
The winds spin yarns of lands unknown.
In every swirl, a voice so clear,
The gales bring forth what we hold dear.

# Silhouettes in the Skylight

Figures dance in evening's light,
Framed against the stars so bright.
Shadows play on wall and floor,
In quiet whispers, they implore.

With every move, a story's spun,
In the glow of setting sun.
A ballet of dreams, both dark and clear,
In this moment, we draw near.

The night unfolds its velvet cloak,
In silhouettes, we start to joke.
In laughter shared, our worries fade,
In whispered secrets, bonds are made.

So gather close, let shadows weave,
The tales of life we all believe.
In the stillness, our hearts ignite,
In the beauty found, we find our light.

# The Dance of Wandering Thoughts

Thoughts like whispers drifting free,
In the corners of my mind, they flee.
They twirl and spin, a graceful ballet,
In the quiet night, they softly sway.

Some linger long, like evening's dew,
While others dance away from view.
An ebb and flow, a gentle tide,
In this waltz of dreams, I confide.

Through fleeting moments, questions rise,
A tapestry of how and why.
In every beat, a spark ignites,
Guiding the heart through starry nights.

So let them drift, those thoughts unbound,
In their dance, a truth is found.
Embracing all, both dark and light,
In wandering thoughts, we take our flight.

# Floating on the Silent Gales

Gentle whispers in the night,
Stars above, a distant light,
Waves that lap with soft refrain,
Nature sings, a sweet campaign.

Clouds drift by, like dreams set free,
Carried off by currents, we
Float away on hopes so bright,
Hearts entwined until the light.

The moon reflects on tranquil seas,
Every sigh, a gentle breeze,
In this space where souls ignite,
Floating on, it's pure delight.

## The Wind's Tender Embrace

Through the trees, the breezes sway,
Caressing leaves in sweet ballet,
A soft touch on skin so bare,
In the wind, a lover's care.

It speaks of tales both old and new,
Of distant lands and skies so blue,
Carrying whispers of the past,
In its arms, we're bound to last.

With every gust, a secret shared,
Lightly floating, none compared,
A dance of freedom, soul set free,
In the wind's embrace, just you and me.

### Flights of Fancy at Dusk

As daylight fades, the colors blend,
Hues of orange, pink, transcend,
Birds take flight, in patterns bold,
Stories of adventure told.

The horizon calls, the stars align,
In twilight's glow, our dreams entwine,
With every beat, our spirits soar,
In the dusk, we long for more.

Whispers echo through the trees,
Carried softly by the breeze,
In this moment, all is right,
Flights of fancy shared at night.

## Sails of the Soul

Set your sails in winds so fair,
Let your spirit wander there,
On oceans vast, beyond the shore,
Find the dreams you can explore.

Drifting gently, waves will guide,
Tides of fortune, side by side,
With each heartbeat, feel the pull,
Through the currents, sails will lull.

In the heart where passions blaze,
Chart a course through life's maze,
With every breath, your story's spun,
Sails of the soul, you have begun.

# Flight of the Lyric Wind

Whispers weave through the trees,
Carried by the gentle breeze.
Notes of joy fill the air,
Melodies without a care.

Dancing leaves in the sunlight,
Twirling dreams take their flight.
In the sky, birds sing free,
Echoes of harmony.

Clouds drift by, soft and white,
Cascades of pure delight.
Across the blue, a sweet flight,
Hearts embrace the warm light.

Winds of change softly blow,
Guiding souls where they go.
With each note, a heart finds home,
In the skies, forever roam.

# Tempest of Springtime Wishes

Thunder rolls in the night air,
Beneath the rain, dreams lay bare.
Flashes of light ignite the sky,
As blossoms wake with a sigh.

Soft petals dance in the wind,
Whispers of hope they send.
Fresh scents of earth arise,
Painting colors in the skies.

Birds take flight in joyful tunes,
Singing soft under the moons.
Life awakens all around,
In the chaos, joy is found.

Tempests pass, but hearts stay true,
In each storm, the sun breaks through.
Springtime wishes take their place,
In the heart, a warm embrace.

# Veils of Softly Swaying Ideas

Ideas flutter like light leaves,
Caught in webs that the mind weaves.
Each thought a breeze of delight,
Guiding dreams into the night.

Whispers call from shadows deep,
Where the wisest secrets sleep.
A tapestry of intent,
In subtle hues, they are sent.

Swaying softly, they take form,
Nurtured in a thought-storm.
Rippling through the silent space,
Ideas dance with gentle grace.

Let them flow like gentle streams,
Into the realm of shared dreams.
In this hush, let voices blend,
Every thought a message penned.

## A Journey through Gossamer Dreams

In the twilight, dreams do weave,
Soft as whispers, believe.
Gossamer threads of the night,
Guide the soul towards the light.

Floating on silver beams,
Each heart sings of gentle dreams.
Stars illuminate the way,
In the dark, they softly play.

Winding paths through silent streams,
Every turn held in our dreams.
With each step, a new surprise,
Magic glimmers in our eyes.

Journey forth on wings of air,
Into realms beyond compare.
In this dance, forever roam,
Finding always, a way home.

# Whispers of the Zephyr

In the soft light, shadows play,
Gentle breezes dance and sway.
Leaves converse in a silent song,
Nature's whispers, where we belong.

Carrying dreams on wings so light,
Stories woven from day to night.
The heart listens with open ears,
To the secrets of laughter and tears.

Above the trees, the sky unfolds,
A tapestry of vibrant golds.
Each breeze a touch, a brief embrace,
In that hush, we find our place.

With every gust, the world will sigh,
Echoing hopes as they drift by.
In the zephyr's arms, we find belief,
In whispers soft, we seek relief.

# Constellations of Thought

Stars ignite in the mind's expanse,
Galaxies swirl in a cosmic dance.
Ideas tumble and take their flight,
Illuminating the endless night.

Each spark a dream yet to be known,
Fragments of hearts, like seeds are sown.
The universe holds each sigh and thrill,
As we ponder, our spirits fill.

In time and space, where moments hitch,
We trace the lines of the thoughts we stitch.
Deep in our souls, the echoes ring,
The constellations, our hearts do bring.

Navigating through the dark we roam,
Finding solace in thoughts we own.
As the night sky reveals its art,
Constellations dance within the heart.

# Echoes in the Night Sky

Whispers linger in the evening air,
Echoes of dreams float everywhere.
Stars bear witness to silent pleas,
Filling the void with gentle ease.

Moonlit paths where shadows creep,
In the stillness, the world does sleep.
Every twinkle a story told,
Of hopes and wishes, brave and bold.

Darkness cradles the hearts that yearn,
In distant lights, we find our turn.
As echoes blend in the vast expanse,
We seek the magic in a trance.

Beneath the sky, we lift our gaze,
In the night's embrace, our spirits blaze.
With every echo that passes by,
We come alive in the night sky.

## Chasing the Celestial Breeze

With eyes uplifted, we feel the air,
A gentle current that leads us there.
Through fields where wildflowers sway,
We chase the breeze through night and day.

It whispers secrets from far-off lands,
Curling 'round our eager hands.
In its dance, we find our way,
A haunting tune that longs to stay.

Clouds drift slowly, painted bright,
Carried along by the fading light.
As the stars beckon, we follow near,
In the celestial gale, we shed our fear.

Together we soar with dreams unbound,
On winds of wonder, we are found.
Chasing the breeze, both wild and free,
In every gust, we find our plea.

## Journeying Through Whispered Currents

On a river where silence breathes,
Carrying tales of forgotten trees,
Moments drift like soft, warm sighs,
Beneath the watchful, open skies.

In the depths where shadows swirl,
Mysteries dance, gently unfurl,
With every ripple, hopes set free,
Charting paths through eternity.

Echoed whispers guide our way,
Through the night and into day,
Stars above weave dreams so bright,
Leading us to endless light.

With each bend, new worlds await,
Adventures longing to create,
Tides of fate pull us along,
In this journey, we belong.

# Notes in the Choreography of Clouds

Clouds perform in silvered hues,
Sketching stories, lighting clues,
Gentle waltz across the sky,
Whispers soft as breezes sigh.

In the canvas of the blue,
A palette rich, a dancer's cue,
Each formation tells a tale,
A fleeting wish to ride the gale.

Moments freeze in soft embrace,
Time eludes in this vast space,
A symphony of white and gray,
Painting dreams that drift away.

Together they weave a song,
A harmony where we belong,
Nature's rhythm, light and free,
In the clouds, our spirits see.

# A Symphony of Invisible Threads

Tangled whispers, soft and light,
Woven dreams take graceful flight,
Each connection, subtle, grand,
A tapestry made by unseen hands.

In the silence, secrets hum,
Notes of life in twilight's drum,
Bound by fate and woven tight,
Invisible threads shine through the night.

Hearts entwined in a gentle dance,
Sharing glances, a fleeting chance,
Echoes of laughter fill the air,
In this symphony, we lay bare.

Time is but a fragile weave,
Moments linger, hearts believe,
In every note, a story glows,
A symphony of love that flows.

## Dreams that Flit and Flutter

In the twilight, shadows play,
Dreams awaken, drift away,
Whispers soft like petals fall,
Catching the heart's silent call.

Butterflies in the evening light,
Flit and flutter, take to flight,
Chasing stars with vibrant wings,
In the night, a promise sings.

Through the garden of our mind,
Wonders wait, so sweetly kind,
Every dream a fleeting spark,
Guiding us through the dark.

As dawn breaks, they softly fade,
Yet in memory, they've stayed,
A dance of light, a soft embrace,
Dreams linger in time and space.

## The Soft Touch of Evening Whispers

The sky fades to a gentle hue,
Stars peek out, a shimmering view.
Shadows dance on the soft ground,
As night breathes life, without a sound.

Cool winds carry secrets afar,
Whispers linger like a shooting star.
The moon embraces the world so bright,
Guiding hearts through the velvet night.

# A Tapestry of Floating Hopes

Threads of dreams in colors bold,
Woven tales yet to unfold.
Each stitch sings of aspirations high,
Kites of wishes on winds that fly.

Sunrise hues paint the canvas grand,
Brightening paths where we take our stand.
In every heartbeat, stories live,
In this tapestry, love's threads forgive.

## Currents of Forgotten Dreams

In the silence, echoes call,
Faded hopes that rise and fall.
Forgotten whispers in the stream,
Flowing softly, like a dream.

Carried gently, like drifting leaves,
Past the shadows, the heart believes.
Where memory and time entwine,
Currents chase what once was mine.

## Ethereal Voices in Motion

In twilight's glow, voices blend,
Carried by winds, they twist and wend.
Songs of ages, tender and light,
Ethereal echoes whisper at night.

Steps in rhythm, a dance divine,
Magic weaves through the silent line.
Each note a promise, each sound a chance,
Together we sway in this cosmic dance.

## Enchanted Echoes Beneath the Stars

Whispers dance in night's embrace,
Beneath the moon's soft silver grace.
Dreams take flight on starlit beams,
Carried forth on whispered dreams.

A tapestry of shimmering light,
Guiding hearts through velvet night.
Lunar secrets softly sigh,
Echoing where hopes comply.

In the stillness, time stands still,
Every heartbeat a gentle thrill.
Magic swirls in twilight's glow,
Eternity drifts, ebb and flow.

Awake beneath the vast expanse,
Lost in the timeless cosmic dance.
Echoes linger, soft and near,
Enchanting whispers, sweet and clear.

# The Magic of Floating Longings

Winds carry dreams like dandelion seeds,
Floating through the air, fulfilling needs.
Yearning hearts on gentle waves,
Caught in magic, the soul braves.

The horizon calls, a distant hue,
Where wishes blend with the morning dew.
Beneath each cloud, new hopes arise,
Floating longings fill the skies.

Canvas painted in shades of desire,
Each stroke ignites an inner fire.
Love and laughter, hopes that soar,
Crafting dreams forevermore.

In this realm where spirits sigh,
Breath of wonder as they fly.
The magic stirs with every breeze,
Floating longings put to ease.

# Threads Woven with Celestial Breath

Stars entwined in a cosmic thread,
Whispers of the universe, softly spread.
Each heartbeat a song, softly sung,
Woven tales through time have spun.

In the fabric of the night sky,
Dreams and destinies wander by.
Silken strands of stardust weave,
A tapestry of what we believe.

Emotions dance in vibrant hues,
Every thread connects the clues.
Celestial breath creates our fate,
Intertwined dreams resonate.

With each moment, the tapestry grows,
In the silence, a melody flows.
Threads of wonder light the night,
Woven wishes take their flight.

## Pulse of the Airborne Imagination

Ideas drift like whispers of air,
Carried forth without a care.
Floating thoughts and dreams collide,
In the realm where hopes abide.

Echoes spark with vibrant grace,
Painting visions in endless space.
The pulse of dreams beats wild and free,
Stirring depths of creativity.

Each heartbeat aches to break anew,
Imagination's dance, a vivid view.
With every thought, the skies expand,
Artistry flows from a gentle hand.

In the air, a current flows,
Where the seed of inspiration grows.
The pulse quickens in twilight's embrace,
Airborne visions, a boundless chase.

# Notes from the Horizon

The sun dips low, a canvas bright,
Colors blend in soft twilight.
Whispers travel on the breeze,
Carrying dreams among the trees.

Stars awaken, one by one,
Their twinkling tales, a race begun.
Night unfolds its velvet cloak,
Each heartbeat holds a silent joke.

Waves crash gently on the shore,
Rhythms echo, forevermore.
Footprints vanish in the sand,
Time slips softly from our hand.

In the distance, shadows play,
Guiding thoughts that drift away.
Notes of life in every sigh,
Horizon whispers, floating high.

# The Song of Unspoken Thoughts

In quiet corners, voices hide,
Words unspoken, hearts confide.
Echoes dance in muffled tones,
Linger softly, like tender stones.

Beneath the surface, feelings flow,
Silent verses, deep and slow.
A melody, complex and sweet,
Yearns for ears that long to meet.

Eyes reveal what lips don't say,
In the shadows, thoughts on display.
Each glance woven into a tune,
Crescendoing 'neath the silver moon.

Time stands still as souls connect,
In the silence, love reflects.
The song plays on, forever bright,
In the hush, shines pure delight.

# Whirlwinds of Inspiration

In the chaos, sparks take flight,
Ideas whirl in vibrant light.
Passion burns in every heart,
Creativity, a work of art.

Words collide in joyful dance,
Each twist and turn, a fleeting chance.
Visions twirl, like autumn leaves,
In the winds, the spirit weaves.

Brush strokes splatter, colors blend,
An open mind, the perfect friend.
Fleeting moments, caught with grace,
Inspiration finds its place.

With every gust, new paths appear,
Horizon wide, devoid of fear.
Embrace the storms that life imparts,
Whirlwinds echo in our hearts.

# Sighs of the Evening Light

As daylight fades, a gentle sigh,
The sky blushes, a soft goodbye.
Shadows stretch and caress the ground,
In twilight's arms, solace is found.

Crickets chirp a quiet serenade,
Nature weaves a deep cascade.
The moon peeks out, a silver plea,
Inviting dreams to dance so free.

Stars emerge, a twinkling sigh,
Whispers of night, lifting high.
Each flicker tells a tale untold,
In every light, a memory to hold.

Embrace the magic of the night,
Let go of worries, take to flight.
In the embrace of evening light,
Find peace within the hush of night.

# Enigmas of the Open Sky

Beneath the vast and endless dome,
Stars whisper secrets, calling home.
In shadows play, the night unfolds,
A canvas rich, with stories told.

Moonlight dances on the sea,
Echoing dreams of what might be.
In silence thick, the heart will sway,
Unraveling threads of night and day.

The breeze carries a distant tune,
A symphony of night and moon.
In twilight's hold, the world turns slow,
Where mysteries of the sky will glow.

What lies beyond this cosmic frame?
An endless quest, a yearning flame.
With every glance, new wonders rise,
Enigmas float in open skies.

# Shifting Clouds of Contemplation

Clouds drift softly, thoughts take flight,
In fleeting shapes they dance with light.
A whisper of dreams upon the air,
Ephemeral visions, beyond compare.

Time flows gently through the haze,
Moments captured in a daze.
Each shadow holds a fleeting thought,
In solitude, reflections caught.

Colors mingle, soft and bright,
An artist's brush in fading light.
In the sky's embrace, we find peace,
As worries fade and worries cease.

Within each shape, a story lies,
A shifting tale that never dies.
Through clouds of thought, we rise and fall,
Finding solace in it all.

# Luminous Paths Unseen

Beyond the darkness, light will gleam,
A path unfolding, like a dream.
In hushed tones, the stars align,
Luminous trails, a sacred sign.

With every step, the unknown calls,
As shadows fade and courage sprawls.
In the silence, clarity grows,
A dance of light, where wisdom flows.

Each heartbeat echoes, soft and clear,
Guiding souls to draw them near.
Through tangled woods and foggy streams,
We walk the path of hidden dreams.

Though veiled in mist, our sight will find,
The luminous threads of fate entwined.
As we journey, truth shall shine,
Illuminating paths divine.

## Drifting Through the Cosmic Fabric

In woven threads of space and time,
We wander free, our spirits climb.
Galaxies twinkle, far and wide,
A tapestry where dreams abide.

Nebulas whisper, winds of grace,
Through cosmic realms, we softly trace.
Each star a note in nature's song,
A fleeting journey where we belong.

Close your eyes, let go of fears,
Embrace the magic, shed your tears.
In the fabric of the night, we weave,
A dance of light, in dreams, believe.

With every heartbeat, closer drawn,
A symphony at the break of dawn.
Through endless night, our souls will flow,
Drifting where the starlit rivers go.

# Soaring Through Starry Veils

Under the vast expanse of night,
Dreams take flight like stars in sight.
Whispers of the wind softly call,
Cradling hopes, we dare to sprawl.

With every breath, we rise and glide,
Through shimmering paths where wonders reside.
Eclipsing doubts, we embrace the thrill,
In the cosmos, time stands still.

Veils of twilight weave a tale,
Adventures beckon from beyond the pale.
In the dance of the moonlit glow,
We find the courage to let go.

Soaring high, we chase our dreams,
In the magic of starlit beams.
Together we shall drift and weave,
In the night, we truly believe.

## A Symphony of Airborne Aspirations

Floating high on whispered dreams,
The world below is not what it seems.
Each gust carries our hopes so clear,
In the symphony, our spirits cheer.

Clouds become our gentle stage,
As we write tales of every age.
With hearts aligned to the skies' embrace,
We seek the thrill in every trace.

The winds compose a vibrant tune,
Dancing softly beneath the moon.
Notes of joy, they rise and fall,
In harmony, we hear the call.

Soaring through the endless blue,
Our aspirations strong and true.
We chase the dawn with open arms,
In this symphony, we find our charms.

# Wishes Adrift in Twilight

In twilight's glow, our wishes drift,
Carried gently, a timely gift.
Stars awaken, shimmering bright,
They guide us through the velvet night.

Each wish a spark in the cosmic sea,
Flowing freely, wild and free.
As shadows dance on the earth below,
In dreams, we find our true bestow.

Soft whispers travel through the air,
Carving paths of hope and care.
Together, we paint the evening sky,
In silent wonder, we all lie.

Through this twilight, we weave our fates,
With open hearts, we hope and wait.
For every wish, a chance to rise,
As love and dreams light up the skies.

# Enchanted by the Sky

Upon a breeze, we feel the call,
The sky embraces, welcoming all.
With eyes wide open, we seek the light,
In this magic that takes flight.

Colors blend as the sun descends,
A canvas where reality bends.
Hearts are lifted, spirits soar,
With every moment, we crave more.

Eagles glide, a dance of grace,
In the heavens, we find our place.
Each heartbeat echoes a silent song,
In the embrace where we belong.

Enchanted, we roam beneath the vast,
In the sky's arms, our doubts are cast.
With every glance, we rise anew,
In this wonder, our dreams come true.

# Threads of the Hypnotic Breeze

In twilight's gentle, soft caress,
A breeze weaves tales, a whispered dress.
Through fields of gold, it dances free,
Threads of dreams in harmony.

Cool shadows play on forest floors,
A symphony behind closed doors.
Where secrets hide in nature's ease,
Intertwined in the hypnotic breeze.

Each sigh and flutter, nature's song,
Inviting hearts where they belong.
With every gust, a sacred tease,
We find ourselves in the hypnotic breeze.

So let us linger, let us drift,
Embraced by whispers, a loving gift.
In every wisp, our spirits seize,
The magic found in the hypnotic breeze.

# The Essence of the Unseen Voyage

In silent depths where echoes wane,
A journey starts from joy and pain.
With every heartbeat, maps unfold,
Stories are painted, whispered gold.

Through endless seas, horizons blend,
We chase the light, where shadows end.
Every wave a tale of old,
The essence of the brave and bold.

In twilight hues, the stars ignite,
Guiding souls through velvet night.
We sail on dreams, our sails unfurled,
On this unseen voyage, we find our world.

Each star a compass, shining bright,
Through whispered winds, we take flight.
The essence calls us, wild and free,
Onward we go, eternally.

# Whispers of the Zephyr

Among the leaves, the zephyr treads,
A soft embrace as silence spreads.
Its voice a gentle, flowing stream,
In every breath, a secret dream.

Through meadow's grace, and mountain high,
It paints the clouds in a sapphire sky.
Echoes linger, a soft reprise,
Every moment, the zephyr sighs.

With every rustle, nature's voice,
Calls to the heart, invites the choice.
To dance with whispers, be at ease,
In the gentle arms of the zephyr's breeze.

So close your eyes, let stillness reign,
And feel the whispers, soft as rain.
In tender moments, we find our keys,
Unlocking worlds with the zephyr's pleas.

# Floating Reveries

In dreams we drift on cotton clouds,
Where hopes are whispered, loud and proud.
Each thought a feather, soft, sublime,
Floating reveries, lost in time.

As starlit nights embrace our glow,
We find the paths that ebb and flow.
With every pulse, our spirits rise,
A dance of echoes in midnight skies.

Through silken threads of faded light,
We navigate the realms of night.
Each heart a lantern, guiding lines,
Floating reveries through endless signs.

So let us soar, unbound, and free,
In the embrace of our fantasy.
In every dream, the world unweaves,
The magic found in floating reveries.

## Echoes of Distant Horizons

Whispers of the evening light,
Glimmers dance upon the sea,
Carried gently through the night,
They call out, beckoning me.

Mountains rise to touch the sky,
Veils of mist that drape the land,
Underneath the stars I sigh,
In this stillness, dreams expand.

Tides of time, they ebb and flow,
Secrets linger in the breeze,
With each wave, new tales will grow,
Chasing echoes through the trees.

In the distance, shadows play,
Mapping stories on the ground,
As I wander, lost in sway,
In the silence, truth is found.

# Chasing Celestial Breezes

Up above, the stars ignite,
Drawing pathways in the dark,
Gentle winds, they take their flight,
Guiding dreams like a lark.

Clouds are whispers, soft and light,
Each a secret held so dear,
Drifting through the velvet night,
Bringing worlds both far and near.

Fingers grasp at fleeting air,
Holding moments not to fade,
In the dance, I feel the flare,
Of a life that's freely made.

Journey on, my heart will soar,
With each breath, my spirit glows,
Chasing breezes evermore,
Where the wild adventure flows.

# Lullabies of the Air

Softly now, the evening hums,
Crickets sing in gentle tune,
Moonlight drapes, the night becomes,
A cradle rocked beneath the moon.

Rustling leaves, they weave a song,
Nature's voice, a sweet caress,
In the stillness, I belong,
Wrapped in warmth, a soft redress.

Breezes hold the dreams we share,
Carrying wishes far and wide,
In the twilight's tender care,
Hope and love in whispers glide.

Close your eyes, let worries wane,
In this moment, find your peace,
Lullabies that calm the brain,
In the air, sweet dreams release.

## Messages in the Current

Rivers flow with tales untold,
Winding paths through earth's embrace,
Carving stories, bold and old,
Nature's script, a timeless trace.

Waves that crash against the shore,
Echo softly, wisdom's call,
In their rhythm, hear the lore,
Of the rise, and of the fall.

Current carries whispers low,
Songs of ages, winds of change,
In each ripple, secrets flow,
Life and time in motion, strange.

Let the water guide your heart,
With each turn, a lesson learned,
In the dance, we play our part,
Messages from tides returned.

# The Flight of Fantasies

In dreams we soar, beyond the skies,
With hearts that pulse in whispered sighs.
Each thought a feather, light and free,
Carving paths in a painted sea.

The stars become our guiding light,
Through realms of magic, pure delight.
Where wishes bloom like flowers bright,
In the canvas of a starry night.

Beneath the moon's enchanting gaze,
We weave our hopes in silver rays.
In this ballet of dreams we fly,
As shadows dance and spirits high.

So come, let's chase the twilight's glow,
In the flight of fantasies, we flow.
The world a stage, we are the play,
In realms of wonder, we drift away.

## Secrets Carried by the Air

The wind whispers tales from afar,
Secrets hidden beneath the star.
Breath of the earth, laden with grace,
Carrying whispers of every place.

Softly it speaks to the swaying trees,
A symphony played with effortless ease.
Stories of ages, both lost and found,
In the rustle of leaves, they resound.

Clouds gather secrets, heavy with time,
Like hidden rhythms, a silent rhyme.
They float above, weaving in the blue,
Carried on currents, as dreams often do.

Breathe in the air, let it unfold,
Each sigh a story, waiting to be told.
For in every breath, there lies a thread,
Connecting the living to the dearly dead.

## Wings of Imagination

Imagination flutters, bright and bold,
With wings of color, stories untold.
It dances lightly on the breeze,
Awakening dreams with effortless ease.

In the quiet of night, it takes flight,
Painting the sky with vibrant light.
Each thought a stroke on a canvas wide,
Where worlds collide and hopes abide.

So let it carry you far away,
To realms where shadows and colors play.
In this paradise, all is clear,
With wings of imagination, we persevere.

Through valleys of dreams, we gladly roam,
Crafting a world, together it's home.
For every whisper, spark, and gleam,
Is the heart's desire, a waking dream.

# A Dance with the Invisible

In twilight's embrace, shadows shift,
An invisible dance, a silent lift.
The air is thick with unspoken grace,
As time weaves magic in this space.

Figures entwined beneath the veil,
With echoes of laughter, a subtle trail.
The music plays softly in the night,
Yet only the heart can sense the light.

Whispers of beings we cannot see,
Guide us in rhythm, wild and free.
Each step a promise, each turn a chance,
To sway with the shadows in a dreamlike dance.

So hush your mind and feel the air,
In this moment, we shed our care.
For in this dance with the unseen,
We find our souls where they have been.

# Murmurs from the Ether

In twilight's gentle grasp, I hear,
Soft whispers from a world unclear.
Fleeting echoes drift and sway,
Carried on the winds of gray.

A chorus sings beyond the veil,
Where dreams and hopes begin to trail.
Each note a story, lost yet found,
In the silence, all profound.

Murmurs weave through starry night,
Guiding lost souls towards the light.
Unraveled tales of joy and grief,
A dance of fate, beyond belief.

So listen close, let silence reign,
For in the stillness, truth may gain.
The ether breathes, a living art,
Whispers that echo in the heart.

# The Enigma of Soaring Souls

In realms where shadows intertwine,
Soaring souls in flight divine.
Secrets hide in twilight's glow,
Where only yearning hearts may go.

Each spirit cloaked in mystery,
Wandering paths of history.
With every leap, they dare to seek,
Unraveled truths in whispers speak.

The sky becomes their sacred scroll,
Documenting the flight of soul.
In every rise, in every fall,
An enigma that binds us all.

Their laughter echoes in the breeze,
A melody that stirs the trees.
In soaring heights, they rise and scream,
In the dance of existence, they dream.

## Beyond the Boughs of Thought

Beneath the boughs where shadows play,
Thoughts flow softly like the day.
Branches cradle dreams anew,
In whispers held, their secrets brew.

Time lingers here, a fleeting guest,
Each moment woven and repressed.
In silence, ponder till the dawn,
Awake to find the day is drawn.

What lies beyond this leafy maze?
A puzzle wrapped in nature's gaze.
With every sigh, the mind will roam,
Finding solace, crafting home.

Explore the depths where musings lie,
Where thoughts can touch the endless sky.
Beyond the boughs, the heart will find,
A world that lingers, intertwined.

## A Saga of Celestial Whispers

In starlit nights, the cosmos hums,
A saga born as starlight drums.
With every twinkle, stories told,
Of ancient quests and dreams of old.

Celestial whispers thread the void,
With each heartbeat, love deployed.
In cosmic dance, the souls unite,
Adrift in dreams of fire and light.

The universe, a tapestry bright,
Weaves fables through the fabric of night.
With every flare, a wish released,
In silence, all that once had ceased.

So let us gather 'neath the stars,
And share the tales from worlds afar.
In whispers soft, our spirits soar,
A saga spun forevermore.

# Tides of Ethereal Thought

Waves of whispers rise and fall,
Carrying dreams beyond the shore.
Each thought a ripple, soft and small,
In vastness where we yearn for more.

Moonlight dances on the sea,
Guiding hearts to places unknown.
In the silence, we are free,
Forever seeking, never alone.

Stars above weave tales in night,
Their glow ignites the paths we weave.
In the darkness, we find light,
Creating worlds that weave and cleave.

Embrace the flow, let currents guide,
For in the depths, our spirits rise.
In tides of thought, we'll bide,
Ethereal dreams beneath the skies.

## Soaring Beyond the Horizons


Wings spread wide against the blue,
We chase the dawn, we greet the sun.
With every heartbeat, visions grew,
In flight, we find the worlds we've won.

Clouds like cotton, soft and white,
Carrying hopes on gentle breeze.
Through endless skies, we take our flight,
Unbound by gravity's decrees.

Mountains fade, the valleys call,
In the distance, possibilities bloom.
With courage strong, we dare to fall,
And rise again from shadows' gloom.

Soaring high, we break the chains,
In unity, we find our voice.
Beyond horizons, love remains,
A boundless realm where hearts rejoice.

# Feathers of Hope

Delicate whispers in the breeze,
Softly falling, stories shared.
Feathers float with graceful ease,
In the heart, a promise dared.

Each one carries wishes bright,
Tales of courage, dreams in flight.
In their dance, we forge a bond,
As the world holds hope beyond.

Colors vibrant, shades of grace,
In the sunlight, hopes collide.
Through every challenge we embrace,
Feathers of hope shall be our guide.

Collecting dreams like autumn leaves,
Together, we will weave our fate.
In unity, our spirit believes,
Feathers of hope will not abate.

# Lanterns in a Gentle Drift

In tranquil nights, the lanterns glow,
Casting warmth on paths we tread.
Floating softly, dreams in tow,
Guided gently where hearts are led.

Each flicker tells a story bright,
Of wishes made beneath the stars.
In their light, we find our sight,
Illuminating life from afar.

Drifting slowly on a stream,
Carried forth by hopes and dreams.
In the quiet, embers beam,
Encouraging our silent schemes.

Together we will sail away,
With lanterns casting golden hue.
In the drift, we find our sway,
A gentle journey, ever true.

### Petals on the Breeze

Softly they flutter, in sunlight's embrace,
Colors a-dancing, a delicate grace.
Whispers of spring, in the sweet afternoon,
Nature's own sighs, a soft, fragrant tune.

In gardens they swirl, with laughter and cheer,
Carried by breezes, no worries, no fear.
A tapestry woven, with memories bright,
Petals on pathways, in soft, golden light.

## A Veil of Clouds and Wishes

A blanket of clouds, draped over the sky,
Whispers of wishes, that float softly by.
Soft hues of twilight, in a gentle array,
Holding our dreams, till the break of the day.

With each fleeting moment, the colors will change,
A dance of the heavens, so vast, yet so strange.
Beneath this soft cover, we linger and scheme,
Wrapped in the fabric of each cherished dream.

## Secrets in a Skyward Gaze

Stars flicker softly, in a vast, velvet sea,
Each one a story, of what's yet to be.
Secrets are hidden, in constellations bright,
Glimmers of truth, in the deep, starry night.

Captured in wonder, we look up and long,
To know all the tales in the night sky's song.
As the world quiets down, we're drawn to the view,
Finding our answers, in the cosmos anew.

## Driftwood of the Mind

Thoughts like driftwood, upon the mind's stream,
Carried by currents, lost in a dream.
Each piece a moment, a memory's trace,
Floating, they wander, through time and through space.

Patterns emerge, from the chaos we brew,
Whispers of wisdom, known only to few.
Embracing the ebb, letting go of the rush,
In stillness we find, the gentle heart's hush.

# Chimeras in the Clouds

A dragon drifts in twilight's gleam,
Soft whispers of a hidden dream.
The clouds parade in colors bright,
As day gives way to tender night.

A unicorn with mane of gold,
Tales of wonder yet untold.
It gallops on the azure sea,
In realms where all minds wander free.

A phoenix bursts in fiery hues,
In skies where sadness finds its muse.
Each fleeting form a fleeting thought,
In airy realms where dreams are caught.

So let us chase these visions grand,
In cloud-kissed realms, hand in hand.
With hearts alight, we'll soar and dive,
In chimera's world, we feel alive.

## Fluttering Hearts on High

Beneath the stars, our wishes dance,
Like butterflies in carefree prance.
With every turn, our spirits rise,
In cosmic blooms, love never dies.

We chase the echoes of the night,
With hearts that sing in pure delight.
Each flutter brings a spark divine,
In skies where all our dreams align.

The moonbeams kiss our cheeks so soft,
And lift our souls, like whispers aloft.
In each embrace, new hopes ignite,
As passion sweeps us into flight.

With landscapes painted in our laughter,
We write our story ever after.
Through boundless skies on wings we soar,
In fluttering hearts, forevermore.

# The Skylark's Serenade

In morning's hush, the skylark sings,
A melody that softly clings.
It trills a tune of purest joy,
Awakening the world, oh boy!

Through fields of green, its chorus soars,
As sunlight spills through open doors.
The flowers sway to nature's choir,
In every note, a spark of fire.

A dance of winds through leaves and trees,
The serenade flows on the breeze.
With every note, the heart takes flight,
In skylark's song, our souls unite.

So let us bask in this sweet sound,
Where music and the earth are bound.
Together we will sing along,
In life's embrace, where we belong.

## Borne by the Gentle Breeze

Upon the wind, our thoughts do drift,
In whispers soft, a precious gift.
Each secret shared a fleeting sigh,
Like petals dancing in the sky.

Through valleys deep and mountains high,
Our spirits glide, they twist and fly.
With every gust, a dream takes wing,
In laughter light, our hearts will sing.

The breeze carries tales of the past,
Of love once lost, of echoes cast.
Yet in its arms, we find our way,
For every night must greet the day.

So let us trust in nature's art,
And open wide each yearning heart.
For with each breath, we shall believe,
In journeys borne by the gentle breeze.

Milton Keynes UK
Ingram Content Group UK Ltd.
UKHW052021251024
450245UK00012B/624